BREAKING THE CODE OF SILENCE

Your Daily Dose Of Inspiration Volume 2
Published by Corlis Nichols
Copyright ©2021 Corlis Nichols All rights reserved.
No part of this book may be reproduced in any form or by any mechanical means, including information storage and retrieval systems without permission in writing from the publisher/author, except by a reviewer who may quote passages in a review.
All images, logos, quotes, and trademarks included in this book are subject to use according to trademark and copyright laws of the United States of America.
Corlis Nichols, Author
Your Daily Dose Of Inspiration Volume 2
Corlis Nichols
ISBN: 978-0-578-92997-2
All rights reserved by Corlis Nichols.
This book is printed in the United States of America.

I am Corlis S. Nichols, a native of Benton Harbor, Michigan.

Author, Speaker and Domestic violence advocate.

During the darkest times of my life, I discovered a love for writing. Writing for me has been therapeutic.

It is my hope, that you will find comfort and strength through my words.

With love, Corlis

In the stillness of the moment, I often reflect on my life's choices and decisions. These are my reflections...

WHAT ARE YOU AFRAID OF?

What would you do if you weren't afraid?

Would you write a book?

Would you walk away from toxic relationships?

Would you start a business?

Would you relocate to a different city/state?

Would you resign from a dead end job?

Fear paralyzes you and keep you stuck in the same position.

Nothing changes until YOU decide to make a change.

Reflection Station

THE MAKING OF A BEAUTIFUL BUTTERFLY

BEFORE THE BUTTERFLY IS REVEALED, THERE'S A PROCESS IN WHICH IT GOES THROUGH. IN THE EARLY STAGES, IT'S JUST A CATERPILLAR.
IT MAY GET STEPPED ON, RAN OVER OR EVEN STEPPED OVER. IN TIME, WITHIN IT'S PROTECTIVE CASING, THE CATERPILLAR RADICALLY TRANSFORMS IT'S BODY INTO A BEAUTIFUL BUTTERFLY.

YOU MAY HAVE BEEN OVERLOOKED, STEPPED ON OR PASSED UP FOR AN OPPORTUNITY TO DO SOMETHING YOU REALLY WANTED TO DO. DON'T WORRY, THEY DIDN'T KNOW WHO YOU WERE. YOU WERE BEING PROTECTED FROM WHAT YOU THOUGHT YOU WANTED.
IT'S TIME FOR YOU TO REVEAL WHAT'S BEEN HIDDEN.

DISPLAY THE BEAUTY OF YOUR COLORS, LET THEM GAZE AT YOU AS YOU FLY TOWARD THE SUN AND THE BLESSINGS OF YOUR LIFE.

Reflection Station

PURPOSE

YOUR PURPOSE IS CALLING.
MANY OF US GET UP EACH DAY TO WORK ON BUILDING THE DREAMS OF OTHER'S. WE'RE OFTEN LEFT FEELING UNFULFILLED AND BURNT OUT.

YOU WERE CREATED FOR SO MUCH MORE. NOW IS THE TIME TO TAP INTO YOUR PURPOSE.

THE PURPOSE OF LIFE IS A LIFE OF PURPOSE. - ROBERT BYRNE

P: PLAN ACCORDINGLY AND EXECUTE.

U: UTILIZE THE GIFTS INSIDE OF YOU. DON'T HOLD BACK.

SOMEONE NEEDS WHAT YOU HAVE TO PUSH THEM THROUGH. YOUR GIFTS WILL MAKE ROOM FOR YOU.

R: YOU HAVE A RESPONSIBILITY TO SERVE OTHERS WHILE YOU OPERATE IN PURPOSE.

P: PERSISTENCE IS KEY. STAY COMMITTED TO YOUR PURPOSE.

O: OPPORTUNITY AWAITS YOU. WHAT ARE YOU WAITING ON.

S: YOU HAVE THE SOLUTION TO SOMEONE'S PROBLEM.

E: EVERYDAY IS A NEW OPPORTUNITY TO WALK IN YOUR CALLING.

Reflection Station

MUSIC

IN MY OPINION, MUSIC SOMETIMES HAS A HUGE INFLUENCE ON OUR DECISION MAKING.
THINK ABOUT IT....

WHEN YOUR RELATIONSHIP IS IN SHAMBLES... YOU LISTEN TO MUSIC. WHAT IF I HAD TAKEN THE ADVICE GIVEN, ACCORDING TO THE MUSIC I WAS LISTENING TO AT THAT TIME .

I PROBABLY WOULD'VE LISTENED TO KEYSHIA COLE AND JUST CHEATED, OR I SHOULD'VE CALLED ACCORDING TO K. MICHELLE BUT I KNEW I COULDN'T RAISE A MAN.

JAZMINE SULLIVAN HAD ME THINKING ABOUT BUSTING WINDOWS OUT OF CARS AND LEAVING MY INITIALS ON THE SIDE. I PROBABLY WOULD'VE ENDED UP LIKE AKON LOCKED UP AND COULDN'T GET OUT.

LAURYN HILL, HAD ME FEELING LIKE NOTHING EVEN MATTERED AT ALL. I WALKED AWAY THINKING, JAHEIM TOLD Y'ALL TO PUT THAT WOMAN FIRST.

Reflection Station

THIS MEANS WAR

AMMUNITION /RIFLES /SLINGSHOT /BOOTS

THERE'S A WAR GOING ON AND YOU'VE PREPARED ALL YEAR LONG.

AS YOU ENTER THE BATTLEFIELD YOUR PALMS ARE SWEATING, HEART PALPITATING AND YOU ARE TERRIFIED.

THE ONLY THING YOU CAN THINK OF IS REVENGE.

YOU WANT THE ENEMY TO KNOW HOW THEY MADE YOU FEEL.

YOU START LOOKING AROUND FOR YOUR ENEMY AND YOU NOTICE YOU'RE ALL ALONE.

THIS IS NOT YOUR BATTLE TO FIGHT.

THIS BATTLE IS NOT YOURS, IT'S THE LORDS.

YOU FORGOT THE MOST IMPORTANT WEAPON (PRAYER)

MAKE SURE YOU ARE SUITED UP AT ALL TIMES.

Reflection Station

THE STRUGGLE

I KNOW THE STRUGGLE ALL
TOO WELL
IT LITERALLY FELT LIKE HELL
YOU PROMISED ME YOU WOULD
NEVER TELL
BUT ALL ALONG YOU WANTED
ME TO FAIL
I TRUSTED YOU WITH MY
HEART
ONLY FOR YOU TO RIP IT
APART
HOW DARE YOU NOT PLAY
YOUR PART
I SHOULD'VE KNOWN YOU
WERE A CROOK
YOU DEFINITELY HAD THAT
LOOK
MY MOMA TOLD ME TO STAY
IN MY BOOKS.

Reflection Station

FACTORY RESET
(ERASE THE HISTORY)

MY PHONE RESET AND I LOST EVERYTHING. MY PICTURES AND TEXT MESSAGES ARE ALL GONE

-YOU KNOW PICTURES ARE WORTH A THOUSAND WORDS. I WANTED TO REMINISCE ON WHAT WE HAD.
-I WAS ALSO HOLDING ON TO THE TEXT MESSAGES JUST IN CASE I NEEDED TO USE THEM AS AMMUNITION TO FIRE SHOTS. (DON'T BE PETTY)

R: LET'S BE REAL. YOU'VE HELD ON TOO LONG. LET IT GO.
E: ERASE THE HISTORY. STOP HOLDING ON TO WHAT IT USED TO BE.
S: YOU'RE STUCK IN THE CYCLE BECAUSE YOU ATTRACT THE SAME TYPE WITH A DIFFERENT FACE.
E: EVALUATE YOUR SITUATION. WAS IT HURTING YOU OR HELPING YOU.
T: ARE YOU THE TOXIC ONE IN RELATIONSHIPS.
(CONTROLLING BEHAVIORS)
(PATTERNS OF DISRESPECT)
(DO YOU HAVE YOUR MATE WALKING ON EGGSHELLS TO AVOID CONFRONTATION)

Reflection Station

PURPOSE PARTNERS

SLEEPING WITH THE ENEMY.

YOU GET A NEW BOO AND ALL YOU SEE IS FIREWORKS.

YOU AVOID ALL THE OBVIOUS RED FLAGS AND SKIP RIGHT TO THE ENGAGEMENT.

BEFORE YOU KNOW IT, ALL HELL BREAKS LOOSE. YOU REALIZE YOU SAID I LOVE YOU AND YOU DON'T EVEN LIKE THEM.

EVERY PERSON YOU MEET IS NOT ASSIGNED TO DO LIFE WITH YOU.

YOU SKIP RIGHT OVER THE FRIENDSHIP STAGE.

YOU REALIZE YOUR VISION DOESN'T ALIGN WITH THEIR VISION.

YOU REALIZE THAT PERSON IS SECRETLY IN COMPETITION WITH YOU.

YOU NEED A PURPOSE PARTNER NOT A PROJECT. (YOU SHOULDN'T FEEL LIKE YOU HAVE TO MOLD THEM INTO THE PERSON YOU WANT THEM TO BE)

THAT PERSON SHOULDN'T DISTRACT YOU FROM YOUR PURPOSE.

Reflection Station

THERE'S A CHIP ON YOUR SHOULDER

HOW LONG HAVE YOU WALKED AROUND HOLDING GRUDGES AND ILL FEELINGS TOWARDS SOMEONE?

DO YOU EVEN KNOW WHAT YOU'RE MAD ABOUT? AT SOME POINT, YOU HAVE TO LET IT GO.

C: HAVE THE COURAGE TO LET GO OF PAST OFFENSES. ADDRESS THE SITUATION AND MOVE ON.

H: STOP HOLDING GRUDGES. YOU'RE ONLY HURTING YOURSELF.

I: IDENTIFY THE NEGATIVE EMOTIONS ATTACHED TO THOSE ISSUES. HOW DOES THAT PARTICULAR SITUATION MAKE YOU FEEL?

P: YOU DESERVE TO LIVE IN PEACE.

Reflection Station

PIECES OF THE PUZZLE

EACH PUZZLE PIECE IS DESIGNED TO FIT PERFECTLY IN PLACE. WHAT HAPPENS WHEN YOU TRY TO FORCE A PIECE IN?

YOU BECOME FRUSTRATED WITH THE PROCESS.
YOU TRY TO CONVINCE YOURSELF THAT IT WILL EVENTUALLY FIT.
YOU OVERCOMPLICATE THE SIMPLEST TASK.
PERHAPS YOU NEED TO SEND THE PUZZLE BACK DUE TO A MANUFACTURING DEFECT. (NO REFUND NEEDED)

STOP TRYING TO MAKE THE PIECE FIT WHEN IT WAS NEVER DESIGNED TO COMPLETE THE PUZZLE.

Reflection Station

LIGHTS, CAMERA, ACTION

THE STAGE IS SET. THIS IS YOUR PERFECT OPPORTUNITY TO SHOWCASE YOUR PRODUCTION.

DIRECTOR: THE STAGE BELONGS TO YOU. YOU'VE WRITTEN THE PERFECT SCREENPLAY.

AUDITIONS: EVERYONE THAT SHOWS INTEREST WILL NOT MAKE THE CUT.

AUDIENCE: ALLOW THOSE THAT ARE NOT APART OF THE PRODUCTION TO SIT BACK AND ENJOY THE SHOW.

ALL ACCESS PASSES: ONLY GIVEN TO YOUR CREW THAT WILL RIDE WITH YOU TIL (UNTIL) THE WHEELS FALL OFF.

Reflection Station

BONDAGE BREAKER

FOR SO LONG, I CARRIED THE WEIGHT OF ANGER, HATRED AND BITTERNESS ON MY SHOULDERS.

AS TIME WENT ON THE BURDEN OF THE LOAD BECAME TOO HEAVY TO CARRY.

THE DAY I LET GO, THE CHAINS OF BONDAGE FELL OFF.
WHAT ARE YOU HOLDING ON TO....

LET IT GO

Reflection Station

UNCOVERING THE MASK

WHAT ARE WE REALLY COVERING UP.

WE'VE BEEN FORCED TO WALK AROUND MASKED. IT HAS LITERALLY BECOME THE NORM.

WHAT HAPPENS WHEN THE MASKS ARE REMOVED, AND WE ARE FORCED TO DEAL WITH THE REAL ISSUES?

REJECTION /FEAR /BETRAYAL /ANGER /GRIEF /BITTERNESS/ HATRED/PRIDE/RESENTMENT/ANXIETY/LONELINESS/ SELFISHNESS/REGRET

IT'S OKAY NOT TO BE OKAY, BUT DON'T SUFFER IN SILENCE.

THE COLORS BY EACH EMOTION REPRESENTS YOUR BOX (LIFE) OF CRAYONS.

ALWAYS REMEMBER, BROKEN CRAYONS STILL COLOR.

Reflection Station

ITS TIME TO CLEAN YOUR HOUSE

AS THE SEASON'S CHANGE, NOW IS A GOOD TIME TO CLEAN YOUR HOUSE.

REMOVE THE CLUTTER AND ANYTHING THAT YOU DON'T NEED IN THIS NEXT SEASON OF YOUR LIFE.

N- MAKE ROOM FOR THE NEW OPPORTUNITIES THAT ARE COMING YOUR WAY.

E- YOU ARE BEING ELEVATED TO PLACES YOU'VE NEVER BEEN BEFORE.

W- IT'S YOUR TIME TO WIN.

S- SEPARATE YOURSELF FROM THOSE THAT CAN'T GO INTO THIS NEW SEASON WITH YOU.

E- EVERYTHING IS CHANGING FOR YOUR GOOD.

A- ACTIVATE YOUR FAITH. ALL YOU NEED IS A MUSTARD SEED.

S- STARVE ALL DISTRACTIONS THAT COME TO KNOCK YOU OFF YOUR SQUARE.

O- THIS IS YOUR SEASON OF OVERFLOW.

N- WATCH OUT FOR THE NAYSAYERS THAT ARE COMING TO DISCOURAGE YOU FROM PURSUING YOUR DREAMS.

Reflection Station

FINAL NOTICE

WALK IN PURPOSE

YOU'VE CONTEMPLATED LONG ENOUGH ABOUT STEPPING OUT AND WALKING IN YOUR PURPOSE.

JUST DO IT!

UNAPOLOGETIC: NO QUESTIONS ASKED. DO YOU!

NON-NEGOTIABLE: DON'T ALLOW ANYONE TO QUESTION YOU ABOUT WHY YOU'RE DOING WHAT YOU'VE BEEN CALLED TO DO.

PERFECTION: YOU DON'T HAVE TO BE PERFECT TO BE USED BY GOD.

BOLDNESS: WALK WITH YOUR HEAD UP AND WORK IT!

Reflection Station

BOXED IN

I'M COMING OUT!

A BOX IS PRIMARILY USED FOR PACKAGING GOODS. IT CAN ALSO BE USED TO STORE IMPORTANT DOCUMENTS.

OFTEN TIMES WHEN GOODS HAVE BEEN STORED FOR A LONG PERIOD OF TIME YOU FORGET JUST HOW VALUABLE THE CONTENTS ARE.
IT'S TIME TO UNPACK AND LIVE OUTSIDE THE BOX.

DON'T ALLOW THE OPINIONS OF OTHER'S TO KEEP YOU STUCK IN THE BOX.

THAT ONE IDEA THAT YOU'RE AFRAID TO ACT ON WILL PUSH YOU TO THE NEXT LEVEL.

DON'T BE AFRAID TO LET YOUR CREATIVITY BE KNOWN.

Reflection Station

OBJECTS IN THE MIRROR ARE CLOSER THAN THEY APPEAR

O: THE OBJECTS ARE ONLY DISTRACTIONS THAT WILL PREVENT YOU FROM ARRIVING AT YOUR DESTINATION.

B: DON'T FOCUS ON WHAT'S BEHIND YOU. GLANCE AT IT AND KEEP MOVING.

J: DON'T JUMP IN ANOTHER LANE UNTIL YOU'VE ASSESSED THE ONCOMING TRAFFIC.

E: EASE UP. DON'T BE SO HARD ON YOURSELF.

C: YOU ARE ALLOWED TO CHANGE THE DIRECTION IN WHICH YOU ARE GOING.

T: YOU DON'T HAVE TIME TO WORRY ABOUT WHAT OTHER'S ARE DOING.

S: STAY IN YOUR OWN LANE

Reflection Station

YOU GOT SUGAR

TAKE ALL THE LEMONS THAT'S BEEN THROWN AT YOU AND MAKE SOME FRESH LEMONADE.
AS I BEGIN TO STIR THE MOST IMPORTANT INGREDIENT IN MY LEMONADE, I DECIDED TO USE SOME SPECIAL SUGAR.

S: STRENGTH
U: UNAPOLOGETIC
G: GROWTH
A: AUTHENTIC
R: RESILIENCE

WHAT'S IN YOUR SUGAR...

Reflection Station

PEMDAS

THE ORDER OF OPERATION.

IN THE GAME OF MATHEMATICS, WE USE THE ORDER OF OPERATIONS IN A PARTICULAR SEQUENCE.
WHAT IF THE EQUATION NEVER ADDS UP? ARE WE ALLOWED TO REVERSE THE ORDER OF OPERATIONS IN THE GAME OF LIFE.

P: (PERMISSION) YOU HAVE PERMISSION TO CHANGE THE GAME. YOU MAY HAVE TO ADD OR SUBTRACT BEFORE YOU MULTIPLY AND DIVIDE.
E: (EVALUATE) YOUR CIRCLE. ELIMINATE ALL NEGATIVITY. POSITIVITY ONLY!
M: (MAKE ADJUSTMENTS) AS NEEDED. MAP OUT A PLAN AND EXECUTE IT.
D: (DEVIATE) FROM THE ORIGINAL PLAN IF NECESSARY.
A: (ADD) PEOPLE TO YOUR LIFE THAT WILL HOLD YOU ACCOUNTABLE AND ADDS VALUE.
S: (SUBTRACT) ALL DISTRACTIONS THAT KEEP YOU STUCK IN THE SAME PROBLEMS.

Reflection Station

PUT ME IN THE GAME COACH

PUT ME IN THE GAME COACH

YOU'VE BEEN ON THE BENCH LONG ENOUGH WATCHING EVERYONE ELSE WIN.

BENCHED: STOP SITTING ON THE SIDELINES WAITING AND HOPING FOR SOMEONE TO DECIDE IF YOU'RE QUALIFIED TO BE ON THE TEAM.

DEFENSIVE PLAYER: GUARD YOUR HEART, DON'T ALLOW ANYONE TO COME IN AND STEAL IT.

FOUL: STOP ALLOWING PEOPLE TO COME BACK IN THE GAME (YOUR LIFE) AFTER THEY'VE FOULED OUT NUMEROUS TIMES.

WINNING SHOT: DON'T BE AFRAID TO TAKE THE SHOT. YOU'VE MASTERED DRIBBLING, SHOOTING AND PASSING.

IT'S YOUR WINNING SEASON!
THE SCOUTS HAVE BEEN WATCHING YOU ALL SEASON

Reflection Station

INSUFFICIENT FUNDS NOTICE

FINANCIAL INSTITUTION: BANK OF LIFE

UNFORTUNATELY, YOUR AVAILABLE BALANCE IN YOUR BANK OF LIFE ACCOUNT WAS INSUFFICIENT TO COVER ONE OR MORE OF YOUR CHECKS. WE'VE NOTICED YOU HAVE RECURRING CHARGES GOING OUT MONTHLY WITHOUT SUFFICIENT FUNDS TO COVER THEM.

PLEASE MAKE DEPOSITS TO COVER YOUR PAYMENTS, FEES AND ANY OTHER WITHDRAWALS OR TRANSACTIONS YOU HAVE AUTHORIZED.

RELATIONSHIPS ARE LIKE A GAME OF BANKING. THOSE THAT CONTINUE TO WITHDRAW FROM YOUR LIFE AND NEVER MAKE DEPOSITS MUST BE ELIMINATED FROM THE BUDGET.

I DON'T CARE WHO IT IS, STOP ALLOWING PEOPLE TO TAKE AWAY FROM YOUR LIFE.

THOSE THAT NEVER HAVE ANYTHING GOOD TO SAY.

THOSE THAT COME TO YOU TO GOSSIP ABOUT EVERYONE ELSE.

THOSE THAT ALWAYS HAVE THEIR HANDS OUT. LET THEM GO.

Reflection Station

I'M PREGNANT

NAME: PURPOSE
THE BIRTHING PAINS WITH THIS PREGNANCY HIT A LITTLE DIFFERENT FROM MY FIRST PREGNANCY. FOR THOSE OF YOU THAT DON'T KNOW MY STORY, MY FIRST CHILD WAS DELIVERED AT HOME. I WAS IN LABOR FOR 30 MINUTES OR SO. WHEN THE PARAMEDICS ARRIVED SHE WAS ALREADY OUT. THIS SECOND BIRTH HAS CAUSED HEARTACHE AND PAIN. I'VE HAD MANY SLEEPLESS NIGHTS TOSSING AND TURNING. I OFTEN WAKE UP IN THE MIDDLE OF THE NIGHT WITH SO MANY THOUGHTS THAT I SLEEP WITH A PIN AND NOTEBOOK NEXT TO MY BED.
THROUGH IT ALL, I WOULDN'T CHANGE ANYTHING. I NOW UNDERSTAND THAT MY PAIN HAD A PURPOSE.

I'VE BEEN DOING WHAT I WANT TO DO FAR TOO LONG.
CHASING A CAREER, THE PERFECT JOB AND STILL UNFULFILLED.

I ACCEPT THE CALLING ON MY LIFE AND I'M GOING TO WALK IT OUT!
THE CALLING ON YOUR LIFE IS CUSTOMIZED JUST FOR YOU.
DON'T WORRY ABOUT WHO HAS SOMETHING TO SAY ABOUT YOUR CALLING.

WALK IN IT.

Reflection Station

INSECURITIES

I GOT LOCKED UP

BOOKING DATE: TODAY

CHARGE: INSECURITY

COURT DATE: TOMORROW

LOCATION: COURT OF THOUGHTS AND FEELINGS

WHAT DOES INSECURITY LOOK LIKE.

SENSITIVITY TO CRITICISM

ASSUMING SOMEONE IS ALWAYS TALKING ABOUT YOU (GET OUT YOUR FEELINGS)

FEELINGS OF INFERIORITY

FEELINGS OF INADEQUACY

INSECURITY DESTROYS RELATIONSHIPS. STOP ALLOWING YOUR INSECURITIES TO BLEED ONTO OTHERS.

Reflection Station

CONNECTION FAILED

OPERATOR: WE'RE SORRY, YOU HAVE REACHED A NUMBER THAT HAS BEEN DISCONNECTED OR IS NO LONGER IN SERVICE.

IF YOU FEEL THAT YOU HAVE REACHED THIS MESSAGE IN ERROR PLEASE CHECK THE NUMBER AND TRY AGAIN.

COMMON CAUSES OF FAILED CONNECTIONS.

(FRIENDSHIPS, RELATIONSHIPS, SITUATIONSHIPS OR ENTANGLEMENTS)

SIGNAL: WEAK, LIKELY TO DROP ALL CALLS.

BLOCKED: THERE IS NOTHING WRONG WITH YOU. IT WAS BLOCKED FOR YOUR PROTECTION.

CONNECTION: DISCONNECT IMMEDIATELY. WHY ARE YOU HOLDING ON WHEN THE EFFORT ISN'T RECIPROCATED.

TROUBLESHOOTING: REVIEW STEPS ABOVE.

Reflection Station

YOU'VE BEEN SERVED

THIS IS YOUR OFFICIAL NOTICE TO VACATE.

DATE OF NOTICE: TODAY

DEAR (INSERT YOUR NAME), YOU ARE HEREBY NOTIFIED THAT YOU HAVE VIOLATED THE FOLLOWING TERMS THAT ARE DETRIMENTAL TO YOUR LIFE CAUSING A BREACH IN YOUR CONTRACT.

YOU'VE ALLOWED

FEAR
DOUBT
WORRY
NEGATIVE SELF TALK
OPINIONS OF OTHERS TO DETOUR YOU FROM PROGRESSING IN LIFE.

FROM THIS DAY FORWARD:

FEAR HAS TO GO.
DOUBT HAS TO GO.
WORRY HAS TO GO.
NEGATIVE SELF TALK HAS TO GO.

SHOULD YOU FAIL OR REFUSE TO LIVE YOUR LIFE TO THE FULLEST: YOU WILL BE HELD ACCOUNTABLE.

Reflection Station

AUTHENTICATION FAILED

BEFORE I POST PICTURES, I OFTEN BROWSE THROUGH SEVERAL FILTERS. I WANT TO FIND THE PERFECT FILTER TO COVER UP MY FLAWS.

YOU SEE, I NATURALLY HAVE DARK UNDER EYES AND I DESPERATELY NEED TO CUT AND COLOR MY GRAY HAIR.

ONE DAY, I INSTANTLY THOUGHT, I AM WHO I AM. THERE'S NO NEED TO HIDE BEHIND THE FILTERS.

HOW MANY PEOPLE ARE WALKING AROUND HIDING BEHIND THE FILTERS.

A FEW THINGS TO PONDER.

CONFIDENCE: ACCEPT WHO YOU ARE AND ROCK IT OUT!

KNOW THYSELF: STAY TRUE TO WHO YOU ARE.

DON'T YOU DARE CHANGE IT UP. SHOW UP FOR YOURSELF DAILY.

GENUINE: YOU DON'T HAVE TO LIE TO KICK IT. REMOVE THE FILTERS AND WALK IN THE ROOM LIKE YOU OWN THE JOINT.

AUTHENTICITY: CHIN UP! YOU ARE DOPE JUST THE WAY YOU ARE. PLEASE DON'T FORGET THAT.

Reflection Station

IS THERE ANY ROOM AT THE TABLE

HAVE YOU EVER WANTED A SEAT AT THE TABLE, BUT YOU DIDN'T QUITE FIT IN.

THERE'S A TABLE PREPARED JUST FOR YOU! SHIFT YOUR PERSPECTIVE: CREATE YOUR OWN TABLE.

YOU WERE BORN TO STAND OUT: STOP TRYING TO FIT IN.

GIVE YOURSELF PERMISSION TO GO FOR IT: STOP WAITING ON OTHER'S FOR PERMISSION TO DO WHAT YOU WERE CALLED TO DO.

GOD HAS FULLY EQUIPPED YOU WITH EVERYTHING YOU NEED.

THE NEXT TIME YOU START TO FEEL AS IF YOU DON'T BELONG IN A PARTICULAR SPACE REMIND YOURSELF.

YOU BELONG AT THE TABLE.

YOU HAVE WHAT IT TAKES.

YOU HAVE SOMETHING THAT THEY NEED.

Reflection Station

STARVE YOUR DISTRACTIONS

DISTRACTIONS OFTEN HINDER YOU FROM BEING PRODUCTIVE AND GETTING THE JOB DONE.

BE INTENTIONAL ABOUT YOUR GOALS.

IF IT DOESN'T HELP YOU GROW LET IT GO.

MIND YOUR OWN BUSINESS.

PLAN YOUR WEEK.

ELIMINATE NEGATIVITY.

SILENCE THE NOISE.

Reflection Station

I NEED SOME JUMPING CABLES

FAULTY: YOU'VE BEEN HURT AND YOU'RE ALLOWING YOUR IMPERFECTIONS TO KEEP YOU FROM GETTING BACK UP.

FRICTION: EVERY TIME YOU ATTEMPT TO MOVE FORWARD, YOU GET HIT WITH SOMETHING ELSE.

STATIC: THE NOISE AND CHAOS FROM YOUR PAST IS OFTEN THROWN IN YOUR FACE.

IGNITE: YOU FINALLY PICK YOURSELF UP AND GO AFTER WHAT YOU WANT THEN BOOM!

YOU REALIZE IT WAS YOU STANDING IN YOUR OWN WAY.

GRAB THE KEYS AND GO......

Reflection Station

WE ALL HAVE TWO OPTIONS. WE CAN COMPLAIN OR WE CAN MAKE THE NECESSARY ADJUSTMENTS TO IMPROVE OUR CURRENT SITUATIONS.

WHAT IS IT THAT'S KEEPING YOU STUCK IN THE SAME POSITION?

~ COMPLACENCY
~ CONTENTMENT
~ MEDIOCRITY
~ SECURITY

Reflection Station

Daily Affirmations

I am in charge of my own happiness.

I love myself enough to walk away from the things that no longer serve a purpose in my life.

I deserve to be treated with respect.

Being me is enough.

Girl, get up with your cute self.

I am worthy of love and affection.

My past mistakes do not define who I am now.

Queen, fix your crown.

Let's stay connected.

 WWW.BREAKINGTHECODEOFSILENCE.COM

 IMBREAKINGTHECODE@GMAIL.COM

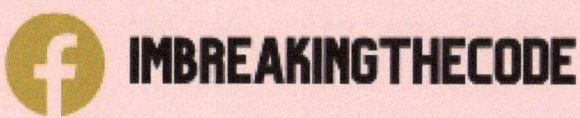 IMBREAKINGTHECODE

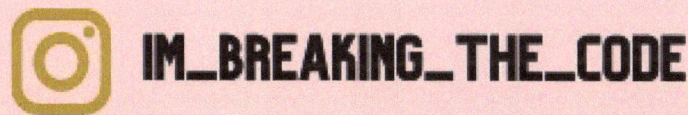 IM_BREAKING_THE_CODE

www.ingramcontent.com/pod-product-compliance
Lightning Source LLC
Chambersburg PA
CBHW041528090426
42736CB00036B/229